40 DAY JOURNAL

TALK TIME WITH GOD

• • • • • • • • • • • • • • • • • • • •

VALARIE WILLIAMS HARRIS

• • • • • • • • • • • • • • • • • • • •

Talk Time with God

Copyright© 2019 Valerie W. Harris

All rights reserved. This book is protected under the copyright laws of the United States of America. This book may not be copied or reprinted for commercial gain or profit. The use of short quotations or occasional page copying for personal or group study is permitted and encouraged. Permission will be granted upon request.

Cover Design by Andrea Huff

Interior Design by S.J. Forester

Published by Final Step Publishing

P.O. Box 1447

Suffolk, VA 23439

www.finalsteppublishing.com

For Worldwide Distribution

Printed in USA.

ISBN: 978-1-7342371-0-8

Library of Congress Control Number: 2019919073

TALK TIME WITH GOD

BY

VALARIE W. HARRIS

Dedication

This book is dedicated to my Lord and Savior Jesus Christ, the source of my strength, in whom I put all my trust.

To my husband, Shurman Harris, whom I love so dearly. He has been my friend, my champion, my rock, and my support system in everything God has called me to do.

To my beautiful daughters, Stacey Harris Robinson (Kevin) and Tia Harris Jones (Lamont), who have kept me grounded, which has allowed me to be me. I pray that they live a life pleasing to God and that they will prosper in all they do.

To my grandchildren, who are the apple of my eye. Loriann, Trez, Kevonna, Jahquan, and Deonte, I pray that, whatever you do, you keep your eyes fixed on Jesus.

To my great-grandchildren Loren, Caleb, Jariyah, Jayla. I pray that you are led by the spirit of God in all that you do in life.

To my godchildren Tamika, Shamika, and Jessica Sykes. Let God be in control of your lives.

I pray that my children, grandchildren, great-grandchildren, and godchildren will love the Lord with all their hearts, minds, and souls as they leave legacies for their families.

To all of my prayer partners and mentors that I have had over the years of my life. I pray that God will richly bless you and your family.

To my Pastor, Rev. Dr. Wesley K. McLaughlin and First Lady, Rev. Pamela McLaughlin, thank you for all of your teaching, guidance and training. I pray that God will bless you beyond your imagination, the sky is the limit.

To my Mount Olivet Church Family, thank you for all of your love and support throughout the years. God bless each of you and I sincerely love you.

Foreword

While this gives me great pleasure to speak on the behalf of the author, Valarie W. Harris, it makes me even prouder because she is my mother. She has been my rock and a mentor all my life as I watched her obtain goal after goal, from childhood into my adult life. She has always shown my sister and me what hard work and determination looks and feels like. She is the strong and rooted pillar in our family, and we can't thank her enough.

Mom retired from Hopewell Public School System after thirty-four years of service, and I knew she would not be able to sit and rest. She was soon embarking upon earning several more titles such as psalmist, preacher, and now writer. As I read through *Talk Time with God*, I was amazed how the Holy Spirit spoke through her in a very compassionate and loving manner. This journal has laid the foundation and presented several tools that will help you navigate the next forty days of learning to talk to God. *Talk Time with God* will guide you down a path of truth. It will allow you to enter God's presence with thanksgiving, praise, and worship while revealing God's heart to you in a manner you may have never experienced before. It provides a heartfelt devotional topic each day along with a daily prayer and surrendering section for you to write down your thoughts and takeaways from the scripture topic.

I urge you to take a leap of faith and devote the next forty days of your life with *Talk Time with God*. Then watch God reveal to you the mysteries of His written word. It will bless you in ways you can't even imagine. *Talk Time with God* is an excellent introduction to new believers in Christ as well as seasoned Christians. It provides you with a roadmap to opening a dialogue with God and allowing Him to minister to you through His written word. Starting your day by communicating with God can help launch you into your destiny. He has so much in store for us each day, and His divine insight, direction, protection, and wisdom can be accessed each day. I pray you will join in and dive deep for the next forty days and experience all that God has in store for you and your family.

STACEY HARRIS ROBINSON

From the Author

Dear Reader,

The purpose of this book is to help you plan your TALK TIME WITH GOD. He is waiting to spend time with you every day. There are times when we need to be quiet before the Lord, asking nothing of him. It is imperative that we learn how to allow our spirit to be open so God can talk with us. He is always talking to us, but are we on the right channel to hear what he is saying? On many occasions, when the disciples were looking for Jesus, he was in a solitary place, spending time in prayer with God. It is very important that we specify a specific time and place to meet with God regularly.

Ask for wisdom and understanding during your TALK TIME WITH GOD, so that you will be able to discern, see, and hear God clearer. Be willing to allow God to rule and reign in your daily life. The Scriptures in this book will cause you to look at yourself and evaluate what you need to do to have a closer relationship with God.

My desire, for you, is that you cherish your TALK TIME WITH GOD. There is nothing like being in the presence of the Lord, exalting who he is and what he has done in your life. Without him in my life, I would be nothing, but with him, I can do all things through Christ who strengthens me. The same applies to you.

Introduction

As we enter into God's presence with thanksgiving, praise, and worship, we will come to the realization that God created us to have a personal relationship with Him. He is the one who initiated a relationship with us from the beginning. We have seen from Genesis to Revelation, that we have been created to worship, commanded to worship, and called to worship God with all of our being, heart, soul, spirit, and strength.

It is all about having an intimate and up-close relationship with God that cannot be matched by any other relationship that we have with anyone else. He is sovereign and all-powerful. I am full of much love and joy when I am in the presence of God. He is the one who put the desire to worship Him inside of us. However, He did give us a choice as to whether we would worship Him. Like Joshua said so eloquently, "For me and my house, we will serve the Lord." As we praise Him, we can pour our hearts out with our most profound affection toward Him. In an atmosphere of worship, we can confess our sins, bow down before Him, let Him know how much we love and adore Him, and show genuine reverence for who He is. We must be obedient and humble ourselves for our worship to be authentic as we prepare for our TALK TIME WITH GOD.

Jeremiah 30:22 declares that God is a relational God. He stated, "And you shall be My people, And I will be your God." This is a declaration from God's heart letting us know that He will dwell with us. So, when we partner with God, our purpose is to love and obey His commands. The only way we can abide in His presence is with His help. We can't do it alone. Throughout scripture, these declarations are revealed to us. If we fall, He is there to rescue us. The Holy Spirit comes through the power of God to reign in and through us. As we become more personal with God, it will remind us that we are His sons and daughters. One day we will reign with Him in heaven. Knowing that we are His sons and daughters helps us to understand that "WHOSE we are, transforms WHO we are."

In your devotional time, meditate on The Lord's Prayer (Matt. 6:13), which says, "For Yours is the kingdom and the power and the glory forever." Just knowing that God has all the power in His hands will help you to build trusting faith. I don't know anyone else who can attest to these powerful words. These words can assure us that God will triumph in His time.

Instructions

Are your ready to spend some quality time with God?

First, we must enter His Presence with thanksgiving, praise and worship, placing our whole being before God. (Mark 12:30)

1. Find a new reason every day to do this. (Prov. 4:23; Ps. 100: 4; 118:24)
2. Present your body as a living sacrifice when you worship Him. (Ps. 63:3,4; Rom. 12:1)
3. Sing a new song to the Lord. (Ps. 96: 1,2; Col. 3:16)
4. Allow the Holy Spirit to assist your prayer and praise. (1 Cor. 14:15; Jude 20)

Second, we must open our hearts, by presenting them to God with confession for cleansing, and diligently seek purity. (Prov. 4:23)

1. Invite the Lord to search your heart. (Ps. 139:23-24)
2. Recognize the danger of deception. (Jer. 17: 9; 1 John 1: 6-10)
3. Set a monitor on your mouth and heart. (Ps. 19:14; 49:3)
4. Keep Christ's purposes and goal in view. (Ps. 90:12; Phil. 3: 13,14)

Third, we must command our day according to the Word of God. (1 Pet. 5:6-11)

1. Surrender your day to God. (Deut. 33: 25; Ps. 31: 14,15; 37: 4,5)
2. Specify your dependence on Him. (Ps. 131:1-3; Prov. 3:5-7)
3. Request specific direction for daily tasks. (Ps. 25:4-5; Isa. 30:21)
4. Obey Jesus' instructions. (Matt. 6: 11; 7: 7,8)

Fourth, we must have the right tools:
1. Bible
2. Bible dictionary
3. Pure Heart of Repentance
4. Stay focused
5. Journal - Make your conversation simple as you talk with God
6. Write out your prayers and petitions
7. Practice by developing a habit of spending time with God
8. Meditate on the scriptures
9. Designate a specific time and place
10. Believe that God is there with you during your TALK TIME
11. Do not allow distractions to overtake your TALK TIME
12. Listen attentively as God Talks to you

As you meditate on each Scripture for the next 40 days, ask God to open your spiritual insight into what He is saying to you. As you begin each day, make sure you repent, forgiving yourself as well as others. Our heart has to be pure in order to receive all that God has for us.

Day 1

Never Depart from the Word of God

This Book of the Law shall not depart from your mouth, but you shall meditate in it day and night, that you may observe to do according to all that is written in it. For then you will make your way prosperous, and then you will have good success.

Joshua 1:8 NKJV

As you meditate daily on God's word, you will begin to desire to live a life that is pleasing to Him. His word will equip us with the wisdom we need to make our lives prosperous. As we experience prosperity, it will allow us to have success in life. Choosing to have success will help you to focus on those things that will cause you to make the right decisions when it comes to your family, friends, church, job, and community.

Joshua was an advocate of teaching the people not to allow the Word of God to depart from them, so that life would go well with them. When we make a conscious decision to meditate on God's word, we will have success just like Joshua did. When we don't apply his Word to our lives, we will end up being unsuccessful and unable to prosper in every area of our lives. The book of Joshua shows the promise and faithfulness of God to His people because they did not allow God's word to depart from them. Joshua declared that he and his household would serve the Lord. (Joshua 24:15)

Your Daily Prayer/Praise:

_____
_____
_____
_____
_____
_____
_____
_____
_____
_____

Your Daily Surrender:

_____
_____
_____
_____
_____
_____
_____
_____
_____

Day 2

SEEKING GOD'S FACE

Seek the Lord and his strength; seek his presence continually!
I CHRONICLES 16:11 ESV

Seeking the Lord, means we are seeking his presence. The word "presence" in Hebrew means "face." Therefore, we ought to seek the face of God because he is the creator of our universe. He is sovereign, holy, righteous, and just. In His presence, there is the fullness of joy, and we can feel His peace. The scripture tells us that when we are weak, he is strong. Remember, as we seek the Lord, we must also ask for His strength because He is all powerful. Whenever we seek the Lord, we will lack no good thing.

Should we only seek God once? Of course not, we need to search for Him continually until eternity. Scripture tells us that when we seek Him, we shall find Him. He is waiting for us to seek Him and for us to desire to be in His presence. We must not allow pride to hinder us from seeking God. Asking for forgiveness is essential to having a pure heart. It is most difficult for some people to experience God's closeness because it involves displaying an attitude of humility, dying to self, fervent prayer, and authentic worship. When we feel convicted by sin, and we repent, it will help turn our hearts back to God's presence. Sin in our lives will cause us not to hear from God when we seek Him.

Your Daily Prayer/Praise:

_____
_____
_____
_____
_____
_____
_____
_____
_____
_____
_____
_____

Your Daily Surrender:

_____
_____
_____
_____
_____
_____
_____
_____
_____
_____
_____
_____

Day 3

Meditating on His Word Makes a Difference

Blessed is the man who walks not in the counsel of the ungodly, nor stands in the path of sinners, nor sits in the seat of the scornful; But his delight is in the law of the Lord, And in His law, he meditates day and night.

Psalm 1:1-2 NKJV

Unfortunately, we live in a society that keeps us busy doing everything for family, friends, job, church, or community, and we omit studying and meditating on the Word of the God. We allow difficulties, distractions, our profession, and many other things to keep us away from delighting in the presence of God. Sad to say, the internet has overtaken many lives. In many churches across America, members are often distracted by social media outlets as opposed to absorbing the Word of God. It is time for a change, but only if you are willing to redirect your focus onto God's Word.

No one can make a person acquire the thirst to delight in God's Word. It has to become a passion and desire from within your spirit. If you desire to have a closer relationship with God, it is imperative that you study God's Word. His Word will keep your mind strong to carry out God's plans and purpose for your life. "Blessed" in Hebrew means "happy," so when we begin to cherish the study of His Word, it will make us happy as well as reflect our daily lives. Remember, studying His Word will never depart from your heart.

Your Daily Prayer/Praise:

_____
_____
_____
_____
_____
_____
_____
_____
_____
_____
_____
_____
_____

Your Daily Surrender:

_____
_____
_____
_____
_____
_____
_____
_____
_____
_____
_____
_____
_____

Day 4

Learn How to Be Still

Be still and know that I am God; I will be exalted among the nations, I will be exalted in the earth!

PSALM 46:10 NKJV

The word, "still," comes from the Hebrew word, "raphe," meaning to be weak, to let go, to surrender, or to release. In our society, we face many challenges, obstacles, and stumbling blocks every day. But we do not need to fret or be afraid of the chaos we witness in the news because God is all-knowing, everywhere at the same time, all-powerful, holy, faithful, and sovereign. We should exalt Him in every circumstance that we might encounter, whether we understand it or not. It is all about trusting who He is. We need to be still by focusing our mind on Him. Once we calm our spirit, we will be able to recognize His presence.

God warned Judah not to align themselves with the Egyptians. They did not take a deep breath, nor did they focus, nor did they listen. By dismissing the warning given to them, they ended up in worse shape than they were before being disobedient to God. They refused to be still, not acknowledging the power of God.

King Jehoshaphat, on the other hand, was afraid of the armies that were coming up against him, so he cried out to God. He gathered the people, petitioning them to pray and fast as they stood still, and they were able to defeat their enemy. When we acknowledge God by exalting his Holiness, we will come out on the winning side every time. Can you remember a time in your life when you did not rely on God, did it your way, and it did not turn out so well? Just know that in our stillness we can be assured to know that God is the only one we can indeed depend on. Our God is a present help in the time of trouble. He reigns and rules in all the earth.

Your Daily Prayer/Praise:

Your Daily Surrender:

Day 5

Wait Patiently on the Lord

Truly my soul silently waits for God; From Him comes my salvation.
Psalm 62:1 NKJV

In life, we will experience many hindrances, some greater than others. David wrote Psalm 62 because of the heartbreak he suffered back in II Samuel 15. He realized that his son had rebelled against him and had plotted to steal his throne away from him. Many of his so-called friends, as well as some of his trusted official, were in on the deceit. It is a hurting thing when your own family and friends betray you. The word, "truly," here in this verse means alone or only. David's soul is silently waiting because only God can bring him out of this situation.

Here, David is confident that God is the only one he can trust to deliver him. He demonstrated trust as opposed to fear, despair, or petition. The lesson to be learned here is that even though we will encounter circumstances outside of our control, we can wait for God to come through for us. No, this is not easy to do, but we can overcome the disappointment because of our trust in God. With Him, all things are possible only to those who believe. David surrenders his heartbreak to one who could handle it. He was not a vengeful man, so he did not take advice from those who encouraged him to take action against those who had done him wrong. He understood that God would allow us to go through things to get our attention. Does God have your attention?

Your Daily Prayer/Praise:

_____
_____
_____
_____
_____
_____
_____
_____
_____
_____

Your Daily Surrender:

_____
_____
_____
_____
_____
_____
_____
_____
_____
_____

Day 6

Trust God in all Circumstances

Trust in Him at all times, you people; Pour out your heart before Him; God is a refuge for us.

PSALM 62:8 NKJV

Trust means to rely upon, be confident, make secure, or feel safe. During your lifespan, you will see and hear many things. It is not wise to reveal specific issues to family and friends because they can be critical, judgmental, and eventually tell others about your struggles. Even to the point of scandalizing your name. In all truth, it is risky to pour out our hearts to people because they will often betray our trust. Proverbs 4:23 tells us that "Above all else, guard your heart, for everything you do flows from it." God already knows our secret misdeeds.

David is a prime example of one who always poured his heart out to God when he was in anguish, distress, or fear. The Book of Psalms is full of prayers that David prayed when he encountered betrayal, pain, and strife during his life. He cried out to God, and He heard his petitions. David was quick to repent for his wrong actions, and that is why he is considered a man after God's own heart.

According to Psalms 142:1, David said, "I cry out to the Lord with my voice; with my voice to the Lord I make my supplication, I pour out my complaint before Him; I declare before Him my trouble." The same goes for us: in our anguish, we can do the same thing David did, cry out before the Lord. We can also look at Hannah in the book of I Samuel, a barren woman who cried out before the Lord, and He answered her petition. She was in so much anguish and bitterness of her soul. Eli saw Hannah praying and concluded that she had been drinking in the middle of the day, but she hadn't been. God was most gracious to Hannah and ended up giving her a son that she promised to give back to him. She called her son Samuel which means "Heard by God." God blessed her with other children after she fulfilled her promise. God is our refuge, and He is the only one we can indeed depend on and trust. Are you trusting God with every situation you encounter?

Your Daily Prayer/Praise:

_____
_____
_____
_____
_____
_____
_____
_____
_____
_____
_____
_____
_____
_____

Your Daily Surrender:

_____
_____
_____
_____
_____
_____
_____
_____
_____
_____
_____
_____
_____
_____

Day 7

That Secret Place is The Safest Place on Earth

He who dwells in the secret place of the Most High shall abide under the shadow of the Almighty. I say of the Lord, He is my refuge and my fortress; My God, in Him I will trust.

Psalm 91:1-2 NKJV

The Psalmist is declaring in this psalm that God is the creator of all things, He is the first and the last, and He is faithful to His creation. Think of a time in your life when you were in a dangerous situation. It could have been when you were out with friends having a good time. You might have been driving along and saw an accident or been in a crash yourself. Maybe you did something you should not have done. Now, as you look back over your life, you see how God protected and shielded you.

These two verses are packed with four different names for God. He is portrayed as the "Most High," meaning Elyon, which signifies God's majesty, his sovereignty, and his pre-eminence. Then he is identified as the "Almighty," meaning Shaddai, who is powerful beyond our imagination: he speaks and something happens, like the parting of the red sea, and he will meet your every need. The "Lord" means either Yahweh or Jehovah. Here he wants to have a personal relationship with you. God will forever be our Father, redeemer, and our friend. He is a friend who sticks closer than a brother. We can find peace, rest, strength, comfort, and protection in the secret place and his shadow. Next, "my God," in Hebrew means Elohim, who is the Father, Son, and Holy Spirit. When all is said and done, we can trust God in every situation we find ourselves in, whether good or bad. He has all the power to rescue us in our time of despair.

Your Daily Prayer/Praise:

_____
_____
_____
_____
_____
_____
_____
_____
_____
_____
_____
_____
_____
_____

Your Daily Surrender:

_____
_____
_____
_____
_____
_____
_____
_____
_____
_____
_____
_____
_____
_____

Day 8

Praise Him with All you Got

Oh give thanks to the LORD, for he is good; for his steadfast love endures forever!

Psalm 118:1 ESV

Every morning should be a day of thanks unto the Lord. In His infinite love, He woke us up with breath in our bodies, a sound mind, good health, food, clothes, and shelter. Who would not want to give thanks for those many blessings? Our minds continually race back and forth thinking about the things we have to do. But we must never forget to thank God for His enduring love.

I don't know about you, but I have had some difficulties in my life, and I have to say that He never stop loving me in my mess. Even though we sin, God does not stop loving you, because His love is steadfast. It is our responsibility to ask for forgiveness by repenting, not to win Him over but because it is the right thing to do. Our repentance pleases Him. Think about this for a moment: as a parent, you love your children, but if they do something wrong, will you stop loving them? The answer is NO. God feels that same way; His love for his sons and daughters will endure forever. Steadfast love is solid, firmly fixed, sure, dependable, reliable, constant, and unwavering. That is how God feels about us. When you accepted Jesus as your Lord and Savior, your heart became transformed. The Prodigal Son wanted all of his inheritance. He lost everything to the point of dining with the pigs. But when he returned home, his father had open arms to accept him back with that steadfast love, the kind of love God has for each of us.

Your Daily Prayer/Praise:

_____
_____
_____
_____
_____
_____
_____
_____
_____
_____
_____
_____

Your Daily Surrender:

_____
_____
_____
_____
_____
_____
_____
_____
_____
_____
_____

Day 9

MEDITATION MATTERS

I will rise before the dawning of the morning, and cry for help; I hope in your word. My eyes are awake through the night watches, That I may mediate on Your word.

PSALM 119:147-148 ESV

In life, we become bombarded with the many tasks we have to do daily. Nonetheless, there are many things that we allow to distract us from meditating on God's Word, such as: talking on the phone, watching TV, spending time on Social Media, online shopping, just busy, busy, busy. I don't see anywhere in this list for spending any time with God. That is missing, and I wonder why?

Ask yourself this question: What are my priorities? Is it more important to do everything you want and leave God out in the process? I hope your answer is NO, but if it is YES, make sure you prioritize your schedule setting aside time to spend in the presence of the Lord. Meditating on God's Word is crucial if you want a personal relationship with Him.

Rising early, before everyone else puts demands on your day, will help you to stay focus on what is most important. You need God's leading daily, so that you won't struggle with being misdirected in your responsibilities to those who care about you. Our quiet time with God is a time that we can cry out to Him for His help, guidance, and the assurance from His Word that we can do all things through Christ who strengthens us. Meditating on God's Word will keep your heart right, give you spiritual success, fill your mind with the things of God and wisdom for direction for your life. I want to encourage you to find a quiet space and to be still to meditate on God's Word so that you will be able to hear Him speak as He directs your path in the way He wants you to go daily.

Your Daily Prayer/Praise:

_____
_____
_____
_____
_____
_____
_____
_____
_____
_____
_____
_____
_____

Your Daily Surrender:

_____
_____
_____
_____
_____
_____
_____
_____
_____
_____
_____
_____

Day 10

The Watchman on the Wall

Unless the Lord builds the house, They labor in vain who build it; Unless the Lord guards the city, The watchman stays awake in vain.

Psalm 127:1 NKJV

A house needs a firm foundation, otherwise, it is built in vain with no way of standing on its own. When we think of a house, in this instance, you will automatically think of family or God's family, the church. If you have a family or ministry in mind, and it is not built on the principles of God, it will not survive. You would have wasted your time, seeing no fruit yielded or produced from your labor.

Scripture, on the other hand, reminded me of the story of how the prophet Ezekiel was called by God to be the watchman for the house of Israel. He was given the mandate to provide them with a warning from the mouth of God. Ezekiel's warning was about their sins and God's punishment to come upon them. It was a message from God, not a word from Ezekiel, warning them about their sinful living.

We live in a society in which everything goes, whether it is right or wrong. We witness for ourselves the ungodliness of man. Our children are being exposed and subjected to all kinds of lawlessness and distorted thinking. They have questions, because they don't understand some of the things they see and hear. Those who do not live by God's precepts and statutes have fallen into the trap of the enemy, feeling they are justified in the wrong habits they are displaying in their lives. My prayer is that they get delivered and set free from the snares and traps set before them.

A watchman's role is not only to speak of sin and the various problems in our society, but they have the mandate to preach and proclaim the Good News of Jesus Christ about salvation. If the watchman doesn't do his due diligence, all their efforts would surely be in vain.

Your Daily Prayer/Praise:

_____
_____
_____
_____
_____
_____
_____
_____
_____
_____
_____
_____

Your Daily Surrender:

_____
_____
_____
_____
_____
_____
_____
_____
_____
_____
_____
_____

Day 11

My Soul Yearns for You

But I have calmed and quieted my soul, Like a weaned child with his mother; Like a weaned child is my soul within me.

PSALM 131:2 ESV

In that quiet place is when your soul can rest as you seek God in His fullness. Do you have time just to set aside everything and lay out before the Lord? In this Psalm, David's brothers accuse him of being prideful, but that was not the case. David was content being a shepherd tending the sheep, but God is the one who calls him out to be a king. In the process, David did not try to be boastful, he waited for his time. Proper guidance led him in the right direction.

David was not seeking a name for himself; instead, he enjoyed that quiet time with the Lord in the field with those sheep. He had a humble heart, and his soul longed to be in the presences of the Lord. His worship was for real. Even though he stumbled in various areas in his life, he never compromised the faithfulness and love for God. David was a man after God's own heart and understood the importance of repenting so that he would not break his fellowship with the Lord. He sensed the importance of staying calm and quieting his soul, because God was the one who would fight his battle when the enemy would come up against him.

In today's scripture, you can learn a great lesson that can help you understand the importance of not thinking more of yourself than of others. Be careful not to be a self-pleaser, instead be a God seeker. Let God be the one to promote you. Pride is something that will get you in trouble with God. When David danced out of his clothes before the Lord, his wife Michal felt he was doing too much, she resented his worship, but that did not stop him from being who God had called him to be. Don't allow naysayers to dictate your worship before the Lord.

Your Daily Prayer/Praise:

_____
_____
_____
_____
_____
_____
_____
_____
_____
_____

Your Daily Surrender:

_____
_____
_____
_____
_____
_____
_____
_____
_____
_____

Day 12

Praise Him

Praise the Lord! Praise God in His sanctuary; Praise Him in His mighty firmament! Praise Him for His might acts; Praise Him according to His excellent greatness!

Psalm 150: 1-2 NKJV

The word praise has seven Hebrew words that describe its various dimensions:
1. Halal which means to boast or rave about God.
2. Shabach means to shout with a loud voice in triumph.
3. Yadah means to worship with your hands extended.
4. Zamar means to sing with musical instruments.
5. Barak means to kneel or bow down blessing God in adoration.
6. Tehillah means to sing aloud in the joy of the greatness of God.
7. Todah means confession, praise, and thanksgiving.

This psalm is a call for everything that has breath to praise the Lord. Here, the psalmist appears to be overflowing with praise on his lips. God is enthroned and exalted in our praise. There is power in praise, and we were created to praise Him. Praise will silence your enemy. It is the garment that we need for the spirit of heaviness. When you think of the goodness of the Lord, all you can do is praise Him with every breath you have in your body. It is not just something to do, it is a command from God to worship with our mouths, our souls, our beings, with the string instruments.

All His mighty acts have been nothing but benefits for all humanity. He showed you His great love when He took all of our sins on Himself giving us a chance for a righteous life. On our own, we cannot even understand His mighty act, His greatness, His power, His Love, His kindness, nor His holiness. He is all that and more. His character exemplifies more than we can even imagine. He is perfect in all His ways.

I don't know about you, but I love to praise the Lord. When you think about praising him in His mighty firmament, it just gives you a glimpse of heaven. As we worship Him on earth, it will be more magnificent in heaven.

Your Daily Prayer/Praise:

_____
_____
_____
_____
_____
_____
_____
_____
_____
_____
_____

Your Daily Surrender:

_____
_____
_____
_____
_____
_____
_____
_____
_____
_____
_____

Day 13

I AM COMMITTED TO YOU

Commit your works to the Lord, And your thoughts will be established.
PROVERBS 16:3 NKJV

Commit means to entrust. It is essential to submit whatever you are doing unto the Lord. When you try to do things on your own, most of the time it will not turn out as you wanted. Scripture tells us that He will teach us all things and bring things to our memory. Often in life, you unconsciously think that you can do everything on your own, but that is not so. God is our source, our director, our guide, the one who will steer us in the right direction.

Be cautious in that kind of thinking. You become disappointed in your strength, because He is the one who will establish your thoughts and give you power. Get in the practice of asking God to direct your path as He shows you the things that matter the most in your life. You would make fewer mistakes in the process. Learn how to be in tune when God is speaking to you about what matters most in your life. He's listening and waiting for a chance to take charge of your works and your thoughts. Whatever you do, God should get the glory out of it. "Trust in the Lord with all your heart and lean not to your understanding, in all your ways acknowledge him, and he shall direct your path." (Proverb 3:5-6)

Your Daily Prayer/Praise:

_____
_____
_____
_____
_____
_____
_____
_____
_____
_____
_____
_____

Your Daily Surrender:

_____
_____
_____
_____
_____
_____
_____
_____
_____
_____
_____
_____

Day 14

Broken but not Defeated

Come now, and let us reason together, Says the Lord, Though your sins are like scarlet, They shall be as white as snow; Though they are red like crimson, They shall be as wool.

Isaiah 1:18 NKJV

For we have all sinned and come short of the glory of God. In this passage of scripture, Isaiah is telling the people of Israel to go to God and repent of their sins. Whatever they had done was not too hard for God's forgiveness. He was willing to turn their sin as scarlet to being white as snow and turn the red like crimson stains back like wool. God was making a promise to them, assuring them that He would cleanse them thoroughly. The same goes for you and me. He wants us to be able to stand before Him as His holy people with no blemish in sight. But by no means will it happen unless some repentance takes place. You already know that your sins deserve His punishment.

Nonetheless, it is essential to understand that you can't do anything on your own. You need help to be steered back in the right direction. You are making a complete turn away from sin by turning in the opposite direction, toward righteousness. Every day of your life you need to repent of your sin, through omission as well as commission.

It reminds me of the hymn, written by Robert Lowry, that we sing on communion Sunday that says: "What can wash away my sin? Nothing but the blood of Jesus. What can make me whole again? Nothing but the blood of Jesus. The only thing that can cleanse us from our sins is undoubtedly nothing but the blood of Jesus."

By now, I guess you can tell that my second favorite person in the Bible, besides Jesus, is David. In Psalm 51, David is repenting after he sinned with Bathsheba. He even asks God to purge him with hyssop, "and I shall be clean, wash me, and I shall be white as snow." Repent right now of your sins so you can be washed clean from your sins. Don't wait, do it now!

Your Daily Prayer/Praise:

_____
_____
_____
_____
_____
_____
_____
_____
_____
_____
_____
_____

Your Daily Surrender:

_____
_____
_____
_____
_____
_____
_____
_____
_____
_____
_____
_____

Day 15

Trust the Peace

You will keep him in perfect peace, Whose mind is stayed on You, Because he trust in you.

ISAIAH 26:3 NKJV

It is beautiful to know that God has promised to keep you in perfect peace. Only if you keep your mind on him will you experience this assurance. The only thing about that is that you must trust in his promises. You will have trials in your life, disappointments, setbacks, failures, rejection, family issues, financial issues, job issues, and friend issues. Through it all, you must trust God to give you perfect peace in those storms of life. It is most important to keep your mind focused on God so that you are able to easily handle various obstacle that you will face.

Remember that our God is a present help in the time of trouble. He will never leave you nor forsake you. As you study God's word daily, you will find peace and rest. That is why it is essential to have a personal relationship with Him. He already knows about your ups and downs; he already knows about our misguide thinking; he already knows about the mistakes you will make. Knowing all of that about you, he continues to be a loving God who you can always trust. Believe that if you trust Him and keep your mind on Him, He will give you peace.

There was a woman who lived alone and every time she tried to do things on her own, she could not understand why there was no peace in the decisions she made. She finally realized that she had not surrendered her total trust to God. Once that happened everything began to turn around in her favor. Today, are you ready to have perfect peace?

Your Daily Prayer/Praise:

Your Daily Surrender:

Day 16

I Know the Plans

For I know the plans I have for you, declares the Lord, plans for welfare and not for evil, to give you a future and a hope.

JEREMIAH 29:11 ESV

It is a beautiful thing to know that, even before you were born, God had a plan for your life. He had a better plan, but instead, you had your plans that you superimposed over the plans of God. He planned to protect us from all evil and give us a future and a hope that would be everlasting. When you do things on your own, not including God in the process, it might work for a while, but the majority of the time it does not last.

Yes, you see the rich and famous who are prosperous, having everything. But ask yourself, do they have everything if they do not acknowledge the one who made it possible for them to have what they have? Are they being fulfilled with the joy of the Lord? Or are they just having a good time in spite of God's goodness?

Israel had disobeyed God, and their disobedience caused them to be taken into captivity for seventy years. They suffered greatly because of their worship of false gods, sexual immorality, paganism, and many other acts, but after the seventy years, only a remnant would seek God earnestly for restoration. Then he answered their petition because of the plans He had for them from the beginning of their lives. Don't get caught up in seeking the wrong things to make it in this world. Seek the Lord for all your answers, and His plans shall be established in your life.

Your Daily Prayer/Praise:

_____
_____
_____
_____
_____
_____
_____
_____
_____
_____
_____
_____
_____

Your Daily Surrender:

_____
_____
_____
_____
_____
_____
_____
_____
_____
_____
_____
_____
_____

Day 17

Pray in that Secret Place

But when you pray, go into you room and shut the door and pray to your Father who is in secret. And your Father who sees in secret will reward you.

Matthew: 6:6 ESV

I want to encourage you, this morning, to find that secret place of fellowship with God where there is no noise or distractions. He is waiting to spend time with you. He longs for your presence. He has much to share with you if you are willing to listen. Prepare yourself to hear what thus sayeth the Lord.

Jesus demonstrates throughout scripture how he left the disciples to find a special place to commune with God. When you start your day off with Him, He can guide your walk, your talk, your mind, your decisions, and plans. When you persevere in prayer in secret, our Father, who sees all, will reward you. In his presence, there is peace, joy, and your creative mind begins to flow. You can focus more clearly. Think about it, can you concentrate when the TV is on, the phone is ringing, people moving all around? You will miss the opportunity to hear his directions and warning for the day. There is nothing like having some TALK TIME WITH GOD.

Your Daily Prayer/Praise:

_____
_____
_____
_____
_____
_____
_____
_____
_____
_____
_____

Your Daily Surrender:

_____
_____
_____
_____
_____
_____
_____
_____
_____
_____
_____

Day 18

Seek God First
Matthew 6:33 NKJV

But seek first the kingdom of God and his righteousness, and all these things will be added to you.

Matthew 6:33 NKJV

In today's scripture, seek means to search for something or make a diligent effort to obtain something. Kingdom represents the blessedness of the followers of Christ, partially attained in this life and ideally in the world to come. As an attribute of God, righteousness means holiness, justice, and rightness. When applied to man, righteousness signifies the possession of Christian qualities such as faith, hope, charity, and conformity of life with the divine law.

You must earnestly seek his kingdom to have the rule and power of God demonstrated in your life. You must pray that God's kingdom will come in the mighty power of the Holy Spirit to save those who don't know him, to deliver people from bondage and strongholds, to heal the sick, and to magnify the name of the Lord. His righteousness comes only through the Holy Spirit, which helps us to obey His commands as we separate ourselves from the world by showing His love towards humanity. Remember, if you seek His kingdom and His righteousness, all these things will be added to you. No good thing will be withheld from you. You must walk in obedience to God.

Your Daily Prayer/Praise:

_____
_____
_____
_____
_____
_____
_____
_____
_____
_____
_____
_____
_____

Your Daily Surrender:

_____
_____
_____
_____
_____
_____
_____
_____
_____
_____
_____
_____

Day 19

Ask, Seek and Knock

Ask, and it will be given to you; seek, and you will find; knock, and it will be opened to you.

MATTHEW 7:7 NKJV

Are you ready to take action in your life to receive God's blessings? Then when you ask God anything, be confident that he will answer. As you seek him, be self-confident that your search will not be in vain. When you knock, believe in your heart that you will be acknowledged, and God will welcome you into His kingdom. Understand that you must act on your own behalf, no one else can do it for you. You must have a personal relationship and fellowship with Christ. You must be obedient. You must persevere, even when He does not respond quickly. If we ask Him, He has assured you through His words that you will receive what you've requested based on you seeking His kingdom, recognizing His love and goodness, and praying according to His will. Remember, it is all up to you. You have to do something!

Your Daily Prayer/Praise:

_____
_____
_____
_____
_____
_____
_____
_____
_____
_____
_____
_____
_____
_____

Your Daily Surrender:

_____
_____
_____
_____
_____
_____
_____
_____
_____
_____
_____
_____
_____
_____

Day 20

God Please Don't Depart From Me

And then will I declare to them, I never knew you: depart from me, you workers of lawlessness.

MATTHEW 7:23 NKJV

In the Bible, lawlessness is often translated as iniquity. The root of all lawlessness is considered rebellion. Scripture defines sin as lawlessness, according to I John 3:4, which states, "Everyone who makes a practice of sinning also practices lawlessness; sin is lawlessness." (ESV) All have sinned and come short of the glory of God. But you have an avenue that allows you to repent so you can get back in good standings with God. Here, there is a distinction with living a lawless life.

The result of this behavior will cause one .not to inherit eternal life. They are betraying someone who has no relationship at all with God. They don't care what anyone has to say and don't want to hear any chastisement from others. They have no moral standards nor do they care about righteous living. This behavior is not only seen in our society today but also in the Book of the Judges. The people did what they wanted to do, how they wanted to do it, and felt right about it in their own eyes.

Don't get into a predicament that will cause you to hear these words coming from God. I never knew you, depart from me. Instead become that chosen race, a royal priesthood, a holy nation, a people for His possession, that you may proclaim the excellences of He who called you out of darkness into His marvelous light. Please don't get caught in the trap of lawlessness. Repent right now, you still have time!

Your Daily Prayer/Praise:

_____
_____
_____
_____
_____
_____
_____
_____
_____
_____
_____
_____

Your Daily Surrender:

_____
_____
_____
_____
_____
_____
_____
_____
_____
_____
_____
_____

Day 21

Find time to Rest

Come to me, all who labor and are heavy laden, and I will give you rest.
Matthew 11:28 NKJV

At times in your life, have you felt burdened with the weight of the world on your shoulders? Sad to say, everyone at some point has felt this way. Working any job can cause you to be stressed out. So it is essential to find a balance between work and family, which is sometimes hard to do. As you know, a family can be demanding. If you are married and have children, and your children are involved in all kinds of activities, when mixed with your work schedule the load may feel pretty heavy. And if you are a single parent, you probably think that darts are coming at you from every angle.

In the midst of all that, you must find time to spend with the Lord even if it is no more than fifteen or twenty minutes. He is the only one who can lift your heavy burdens and give you the strength to endure them. He is the only one who can give you the rest you need to make it through your frustrating times. Make sure, above all else, that you find rest so your soul can be renewed.

Your Daily Prayer/Praise:

_____
_____
_____
_____
_____
_____
_____
_____
_____
_____
_____
_____

Your Daily Surrender:

_____
_____
_____
_____
_____
_____
_____
_____
_____
_____
_____
_____

Day 22

Do It Alone

And after he had dismissed the crowds, he went up on the mountain by himself to pray. When evening came, he was there alone.

MATTHEW 14:23 ESV

Have you ever thought about getting away from the busyness of your schedule to just enjoying some time of peace away from everybody? You are always going from this place to that place, never stopping to think that you need some time for yourself. Take a moment to get in a quiet place without the phone ringing, questions being asked, TV noise, and the chores of life and see what this looks and feels like? When you are so busy, it is hard to hear from God. He needs you to be still so you can listen to what thus sayeth the Lord. Jesus always went away to a solitary place to pray to rejuvenate himself. He needed that quiet time with the Father to get strengthened. Jesus healed the sick, opened blinded eyes, made the lame to walk, freed those who were in bondage, and displayed a spirit of love for everyone He came in contact with. Can you say that about yourself?

Your Daily Prayer/Praise:

_____
_____
_____
_____
_____
_____
_____
_____
_____
_____

Your Daily Surrender:

_____
_____
_____
_____
_____
_____
_____
_____
_____
_____

Day 23

Rise Early

And rising very early in the morning, while it was still dark, he departed and went out to a desolated place, and there he prayed.

MARK 1:35 ESV

Going to work early is one thing, rising early to pray is another. Have you ever been sleeping so well and then all of a sudden you just wake up and can't go back to sleep? That is God waking you up early to spend some time with you before your mind gets to racing about all the other things you have to do during the day. The majority of the time, people miss that opportunity because they don't even realize that God is trying to have that special time with them. Jesus always slipped away to pray, seeking His Father in prayer. If you are already practicing rising early in the morning, that's a great thing. If you aren't, I challenge you, for the next seven days, to rise early with the intention of having some quality time with God. He has something to tell you. Find a special place for just you and Jesus to commune together.

Your Daily Prayer/Praise:

_____
_____
_____
_____
_____
_____
_____
_____
_____
_____
_____

Your Daily Surrender:

_____
_____
_____
_____
_____
_____
_____
_____
_____
_____
_____

Day 24

Faith that Can Move Mountains

And Jesus answered them, Have faith in God. Truly, I say to you, whoever says to this mountain, Be taken up and thrown into the sea, and does not doubt in his heart, but believes that what he says will come to pass, it will be done for him.

Mark 11:22-23 ESV

Think about today's scripture for a moment, can you move a mountain? No. But what the text is telling you is that all you need is faith the size of a mustard seed. And with that much faith, any obstacle that comes up against you can be removed. You must have faith in God without any doubt that your situation will get better. You must believe in your heart that His Word will come to pass. At times in my life, when difficulties came out of nowhere, automatically I tried to handle it myself. I am here to tell you that does not work.

When you rely on God in that place of disillusion, believe me, He can move those mountains out of your way. No matter how tall and wide the mountain might be, He can cause it to fall. He can cause barriers to fall, walls to fall, sickness to fall, financial problems to fall. Through the power of God, we can witness miracles in the midst of the chaos. "Now faith is the substance of things hoped for, the evidence of things not seen." (Hebrew 11:1 NKJV) As you spend time in the presence of the Lord, this reality will become clearer to you. Don't worry and don't fret, simply trust God for the impossible with no doubt in your heart. What mountain needs to be moved out of your life?

Your Daily Prayer/Praise:

_____
_____
_____
_____
_____
_____
_____
_____
_____
_____

Your Daily Surrender:

_____
_____
_____
_____
_____
_____
_____
_____
_____
_____

Day 25

In that Place

Now Jesus was praying in a certain place, and when he finished, one of his disciples said to him, Lord, teach us to pray, as John taught his disciples.

LUKE 11:1 ESV

The disciples were influenced by Jesus' prayer life to the point that they wanted Him to teach them how to pray. He is our best model of someone who took time out of His schedule to pray. Throughout the Gospels, Jesus went to the mountainside to pray, sat by the lake to pray, and withdrew by boat to pray. He walked ninety miles from Galilee to Jerusalem in silent prayer and prayed on the Mount of Olives, which was his usual place to pray. This occurred whenever he was in Jerusalem. It is how he began his ministry.

As a disciple of Jesus Christ, having a prayer life is essential when making decisions, to prepare yourself daily for warfare when it comes to dealing with others. Here in this scripture, it talks about Him going to a certain place to pray. Prayer gives you the power to defeat the enemy, it will bring you peace in the storms of life, and it will help you make the right choices. Prayer should be the lifestyle of a believer. Have you set aside a specific prayer time and place for yourself?

Your Daily Prayer/Praise:

___

Your Daily Surrender:

___

Day 26

Stay connected to the Vine

I am the vine; you are the branches. He who abides in Me, and I in him, bears much fruit; for without Me you can do nothing.

JOHN 15:5 NKJV

If you are not bearing any fruit, check yourself to see why not. Our Father is the vinedresser, Jesus is the vine, and we are the branches. Any branch that does not bear fruit is removed and burned. Those that bear fruit are pruned or cleansed. This point right here caused me to understand that pruning in our spiritual life might come in the form of sickness, hardships, or loss of material possessions. It could even be persecution from believers as well as non-believers. Whatever the situation, I have found that God still loves me and will care for me in the pruning process because He wants me to stay spiritually healthy and productive throughout my life.

Abiding in His presence gives you the extra benefits of the indwelling presence of God's Spirit. His presence assures us of His love for us. Seek to abide in the presence of God on a daily basis.

Your Daily Prayer/Praise:

_____
_____
_____
_____
_____
_____
_____
_____
_____
_____
_____
_____

Your Daily Surrender:

_____
_____
_____
_____
_____
_____
_____
_____
_____
_____
_____
_____

Day 27

God's Power Makes a Difference

But you will receive power when the Holy Spirit as come upon you, and you will be my witnesses in Jerusalem and in all Judea and Samaria, and to the end of the earth.

Acts 1:8 NKJV

Without the power of the Holy Spirit, you cannot witness effectively to others. The harvest is plentiful, but the laborers are few. The disciples went two by two to witness. What is your exercise? Your witness needs to first start in your home with your family, which can be difficult, before witnessing to anybody else. Then to others whom you encounter, in your community or in the marketplace, before you try to witness in the other parts of the world.

Pray before you try to witness, asking God for his help. Ask God to lead you to the people He wants you to witness too. Believe that their hearts have been softened to receive what the Lord is saying to them through you. You can't beat a person down because they are not where you think they ought to be in their relationship with God. They need to feel your love above everything else. Have you witnessed to anybody lately? What are your waiting for?

Your Daily Prayer/Praise:

_____
_____
_____
_____
_____
_____
_____
_____
_____
_____
_____
_____

Your Daily Surrender:

_____
_____
_____
_____
_____
_____
_____
_____
_____
_____
_____
_____

Day 28

Dying to Your Flesh Daily Isn't Easy

For to set the mind on the flesh is death, but to set the mind on the Spirit is life and peace.

ROMANS 8:6 ESV

If you are constantly giving into fleshly desires, you will put a strain on your fellowship with Jesus. You will still have a relationship with Him, but your fellowship is broken when you sin against God. That is what happened to Adam and Eve when they sinned in the Garden of Eden. They experienced spiritual death because they were both disobedient to God. It is so important to learn how to control your flesh, which can only be done with the help of the Holy Spirit. The lust of the eye, the lust of the flesh, and the pride of life will get you in trouble with God.

Jesus was perfect in all that He did, even though He experienced some of the same things we experience, but the difference is that He did not succumb to sin. The first Adam sinned against God, but the second Adam, Jesus Christ, did not. So, when we learn to set our minds on the Spirit instead of the flesh, we will be able to experience that peace in our lives. You have the power to overcome the tactics of the enemy if you make the choice to defeat him. Be strong in the Lord and He will renew your strength. When you feel weak, you must rely on the strength of the Lord. According to Isaiah 26:3, "You keep him in perfect peace whose mind is stayed on you, because he trusts in you." (ESV)

Your Daily Prayer/Praise:

_____
_____
_____
_____
_____
_____
_____
_____
_____
_____
_____
_____

Your Daily Surrender:

_____
_____
_____
_____
_____
_____
_____
_____
_____
_____
_____

Day 29

Take Control of Your Body

I appeal to you therefore, brothers, by the mercies of God, present your bodies as a living sacrifice, holy and acceptable to God, which is our spiritual worship.

ROMANS 12:1 ESV

Learning self-control can be difficult, especially in the area of eating. If you like to eat, for instance, you don't take into account what certain foods will do to your body. So, it is easy to get in the bad habit of eating things that are unhealthy. I am guilty of that. It is all about taking control of your life by defeating bad habits that will cause you to misuse your body. It might not be food for you. It could be other things, such as smoking, drinking, sexual immorality, illegal pills, or drugs, but whatever the case, you must learn to take control of your own body. You must know that when you do abuse your body, there are consequences. High blood pressure will begin to creep in. Diabetes will show up. Sleep apnea will overshadow you. Then you have to assess the damage that you caused. When you look around, all you can say is, look at what I have done to myself. You can't blame the devil because you are at fault.

I am here this morning to encourage you to get control of your body because it belongs to God. Stop indulging in things that are harmful to your body because He desires better for you. My prayer this morning is that God will take control of your mind, body, and spirit, because these unhealthy actions start in our mind and falter to the rest of your body. Rely on the help of the Holy Spirit, who will help you to take control, so you can present your bodies as a living sacrifice, holy and acceptable to God. That is our spiritual worship toward Him. Are you ready to make a change in your mindset?

Your Daily Prayer/Praise:

_____
_____
_____
_____
_____
_____
_____
_____
_____
_____
_____

Your Daily Surrender:

_____
_____
_____
_____
_____
_____
_____
_____
_____
_____
_____

Day 30

Transform My Mind Lord

Do not be conformed to this world, but be transformed by the renewal of your mind, that by testing you may discern what is the will of God, what is good and acceptable and perfect.

ROMANS 12:2 ESV

It is so easy to get caught up in the world's system. When you are inside looking out, it appears to be so appealing. Don't try to compete with other people who look like they have it all together. In reality, they are just as miserable as they can be. They have all the material things but Jesus is missing from the equation. You acquire nothing on your own. It is Jesus who allows you to have what you have. There would be more people in churches around the world if they didn't allow the world's influence and possessions to take control of their lives. On Sunday, people say they are too tired to go to the church, but instead they will wash their cars or go to sporting events.

You can tell when someone has a renewed mind. They allow the leading of the Holy Spirit to guide them into all truth. Do you want to be in the perfect will of God? Don't let the world's way trump God's will, by renewing your mind. Test your actions and discern what the perfect will of God is.

Your Daily Prayer/Praise:

_____
_____
_____
_____
_____
_____
_____
_____
_____
_____
_____
_____

Your Daily Surrender:

_____
_____
_____
_____
_____
_____
_____
_____
_____
_____
_____

Day 31

Pray at All Times

Praying at all times in the Spirit, with all prayer and supplication. To that end, keep alert with all perseverance, making supplication for all the saints.

Ephesians 6:18

Just like putting your clothes on daily, that is the same way you ought to clothe yourself with praying at all times in the Spirit. Praying in the spirit will cover you when the enemy tries to come up against you. Praying for your enemy will bring them to their knees. You must be unshakable in your petition before the Lord. Praying at all times is an opportunity to acknowledge your weakness and your need for the Lord's help against the enemy. Your dependence in prayer must be the consistent attitude of your heart, both in difficult times and prosperous periods in your life, not forgetting your need for God.

Your prayers and supplications are being passed on from Jesus to His Father for approval. You should not only petition God for your benefit but on behalf of others. Pray, especially for those who are lost, that they would find their way to Jesus.

Your Daily Prayer/Praise:

_____
_____
_____
_____
_____
_____
_____
_____
_____
_____
_____
_____

Your Daily Surrender:

_____
_____
_____
_____
_____
_____
_____
_____
_____
_____
_____
_____

Day 32

Stop Being in a Hurry

Do not be anxious about anything, but in everything by prayer and supplication with thanksgiving let your requests be made known to God.
PHILIPPIANS 4:6 ESV

Most of the time, you are rushing around in the morning trying to get this or that done before you start your day. When you become anxious, the majority of the time you will forget what you supposed to be doing. You can't find your keys, or you forget whether you turned the stove or iron off. Don't allow being anxious to rob or distract you from having peace with God. It is time to relax and let God's presence control your mind.

Start your morning off in prayer. Ask the Lord to direct your thoughts to increase your capacity and to direct your path in the way He would have you to go. Intercede on behalf of others, asking Him to watch over them, to protect them, to bless them. You have to let the Lord hear your request. Thank Him in advance for what He has already done and what He is about to do for the individuals you have prayed for. Put it all in His hands and remove yourself from the equation. During the day, as you think of God's mercy and grace, just begin to thank Him. He and His mercy are everlasting. Right now, give God some praise for His greatness. He is worthy of all the praise, so honor Him right now. Give Him your best praise this morning, He's waiting on you!

Your Daily Prayer/Praise:

_____
_____
_____
_____
_____
_____
_____
_____
_____
_____
_____

Your Daily Surrender:

_____
_____
_____
_____
_____
_____
_____
_____
_____
_____
_____

Day 33

Ongoing Conversation with God

Continue steadfastly in prayer, being watchful in it with thanksgiving.
COLOSSIANS 4:2 ESV

"Steadfastly" means to be unwavering, fixed in a direction or firm in purpose. Persevere in prayer and devote yourself to pray and be thankful. In this letter to the Christians, Paul was asking the people to be loyal in their prayer. It was a personal prayer, then it transitioned into a command related to how Christians should speak. He used the metaphor of salt to explain to them what he was talking about. During the time Paul was writing this letter, salt was valuable and could be used as money. It could preserve and flavor foods in the same way that a believer's conversation should be caring and useful. Our interaction should sound nothing like the conversation of a non-believer. Our discussion should only be to preserve the message of Jesus Christ as we pray to be alert and observe our surroundings.

People are watching and listening to you, so be mindful of what you say. It could have an impact, or it could discourage the nonbeliever. Prayer is not something you do just for a special event; it should be constant and an ongoing conversation with God.

Your Daily Prayer/Praise:

_____
_____
_____
_____
_____
_____
_____
_____
_____
_____
_____
_____
_____
_____

Your Daily Surrender:

_____
_____
_____
_____
_____
_____
_____
_____
_____
_____
_____
_____
_____
_____

Day 34

God's Word is Everlasting

Do you best to present yourself to God as one approved, a worker who has not need to be ashamed, rightly handling the word of truth.

II Timothy 2:15 ESV

God's Word is sharper than any two-edged sword. As you learn His Word, be careful to handle it carefully. Paul tells us in this passage that we must work diligently with the interpretation of the Word of God. You must use sound clarification as you study it within the church and with God's people, so you or they won't go astray in their understanding. Be faithful in learning all you can about the Word of God. Whatever you don't understand, ask God. Scripture tells us that He will teach us all things, so don't dismiss that promise. Stand on that promise, believing God will do just what He said He would do.

Your Daily Prayer/Praise:

_____
_____
_____
_____
_____
_____
_____
_____
_____
_____
_____
_____

Your Daily Surrender:

_____
_____
_____
_____
_____
_____
_____
_____
_____
_____
_____
_____

Day 35

Breathe on Me

All scripture is given by inspiration of God, and is profitable for doctrine, for reproof, for correction, for instruction in righteousness.

II Timothy 3:16 ESV

The Word of God was breathed on forty holy men who carried out his plan for humanity. His Word is accurate, infallible, without error. As you read the Word of God, it will cleanse you, convict you, correct you, and chastise you as it shows you how to live a holy life before God. It is the best book I have ever read. Each time I have read it, I have learned something new. I want to challenge you not only to read the Bible, but to study its content for clarity and understanding of what you have read. It is easy to misunderstand what you have read, so it is essential to be a part of a small group bible study.

The Spirit will teach us all things, but he also will use people within your group to bring more clarity to your understanding of the Word. Believing and knowing His Word will give you the power to withstand the wiles of the enemy. It will lift your burdens, help you solve your problems, bring deliverance in your life, give you joy, peace, comfort, and love. It will cause you to live righteously only if you adhere to what God is speaking to you. It will equip you to teach it to others. What you learn is not to be kept to yourself, it is to be passed onto someone else. Will you make a conscious effort to study God's Word daily?

Your Daily Prayer/Praise:

_____
_____
_____
_____
_____
_____
_____
_____
_____
_____
_____
_____
_____

Your Daily Surrender:

_____
_____
_____
_____
_____
_____
_____
_____
_____
_____
_____
_____
_____

Day 36

Your Praise Matters

Through him then let us continually offer up a sacrifice of praise to God, that is, the fruit of lips that acknowledge his name. Do not neglect to do good and to share what you have, for such sacrifices are pleasing to God.
Hebrew 13:15-16 ESV

Bless the Lord, O my soul, and all that is within me, bless your holy name! Our praise matters to God. He alone is worthy and deserves our praise. All you have to do is open up your mouth right now with the fruit of your lips and thank the Lord for His grace and mercy. Thank Him for His loving kindness. Thank Him for saving a sinner like you and me and thank Him for forgiving all of our sins on the cross at Calvary. He did not have to do it, but He did.

Yes, it is a sacrifice to praise God. Think about it, He gave the ultimate sacrifice for all humanity when He died on that old rugged cross. Who wouldn't want to worship a God like that? Can you imagine what life would be like if it had not been for God's love for his children? He gave His only begotten son for you and me. Who do you know today that would do that for you? Today, make an effort to praise God for His mighty acts of kindness towards you. Share the love of Christ with someone today.

Your Daily Prayer/Praise:

_____
_____
_____
_____
_____
_____
_____
_____
_____
_____
_____
_____

Your Daily Surrender:

_____
_____
_____
_____
_____
_____
_____
_____
_____
_____
_____
_____

Day 37

ARE YOU READY TO SUBMIT!

Submit yourselves therefore to God. Resist the devil, and he will flee from you.

JAMES 4:7 ESV

In the society we live in today, we witness a lot of people who claim to submit to God. They go to church Sunday after Sunday, go to bible study Tuesday after Tuesday, and still hate their fellow man. Prejudice is still alive in America. But we are talking about submitting yourself to God and resisting the devil, and he will flee from you. As Christians, we must be aware of the presence of evil.

Yes, it is a struggle to stand firm, but we can stand firm, because of our faith, only if we chose to. But we must understand one thing, and that is the enemy is real. According to Ephesians 6:12, "For we do not wrestle against flesh and blood but against the rulers, against the authorities, against the cosmic powers over this present darkness, against the spiritual forces of evil in heavenly places." (ESV) We must understand that, "The thief comes only to steal and kill and destroy; I have come that they may have life and have it to the full." (John 10:10, ESV)

When you resist something, that means you will withstand, strive against, or oppose in some manner. The only way to combat the devil is by submitting to God. So, when you resist the devil, he knows that he has no power over you.

On the other hand, if you are disobedient or not submissive as a believer, you will not see victory. You might get a false sense that you have won, but it's only in your mind. Don't allow the enemy to harden your heart, because God knows every man's heart. God is love. How can you say you love God, who you have never seen, when you don't love those you see every day? Resist the tactics of being prejudiced, which comes from the devil, and he will flee.

Your Daily Prayer/Praise:

_____
_____
_____
_____
_____
_____
_____
_____
_____
_____
_____
_____

Your Daily Surrender:

_____
_____
_____
_____
_____
_____
_____
_____
_____
_____
_____
_____

Day 38

Draw Me Nearer God

Draw near to God, and he will draw near to you. Cleanse your hands, you sinners, and purify your hearts, you double-minded.

JAMES 4:8 NKJV

How do you develop a relationship with a friend, boyfriend/girlfriend, or spouse? By spending time with them. You begin to have fun with the person, always wanting to be around them. You start enjoying their presence. You strive to have a deeper relationship with them. It is the same with God. James, in this verse, is talking about drawing near to God, and He will draw near to you. When you draw near to God, you can hear Him better, see Him better, and contact Him better. Why? Because you have deepened your relationship with Him. What will prevent this from happening? If you allow the world to come between you and God, your heart will become hardened towards Him, and it will cause you to experience a downward spiral in your life.

You can't serve two masters, because He is a jealous God. Don't allow other things in your life to get more of your attention than God. It's all about coming to know Him more deeply. So, make sure you go before Him with clean hands and pure heart, repenting of your sin. We have all sinned and come short of the glory of God. But all you need do is ask God for His forgiveness with sincerity of heart.

Your Daily Prayer/Praise:

_____
_____
_____
_____
_____
_____
_____
_____
_____
_____
_____
_____

Your Daily Surrender:

_____
_____
_____
_____
_____
_____
_____
_____
_____
_____
_____
_____

Day 39

Forgive Us Lord

If my people who are called by my name humble themselves and pray and seek my face and turn from their wicked ways, then I will hear from heaven and will forgive their sin and heal their land.

II Chronicles 7:14 NKJV

As we look at the media daily, we see wickedness all around. The way things are happening in our nation today, God is not pleased. He has his arms open wide for those who are willing to show humility, those who will pray, those who long for him by seeking him, and those willing to repent. Turning from their wicked ways and coming back to Him is what He is waiting for. When we as a people do this, He would hear, forgive, and heal our land. It is just that simple. You can't afford to play the waiting game to turn your life around, because you will never know the day nor the hour, because things can change in an instant. Please join with me in praying that a change will come throughout our nation.

God loves us and has a wonderful plan for each of our lives if we are willing to walk in the ways of the Lord. Reach out to someone who needs to turn their life around before it's too late. It's time to pray fervently for people all over the world. Are you ready?

Your Daily Prayer/Praise:

_____
_____
_____
_____
_____
_____
_____
_____
_____
_____

Your Daily Surrender:

_____
_____
_____
_____
_____
_____
_____
_____
_____
_____

Day 40

Words Matter

Let the words of my mouth and the meditation of my heart be acceptable in Your sight, Lord my rock and my redeemer.

PSALM 19:4 ESV

Think about a time when you engaged in conversation with someone, and their words were very disturbing. All they did was criticize, complain, and give their opinion about what they thought someone ought to do. On some occasion, we have all fallen short in this area. To please God with the words that we say, they must be: uplifting, encouraging, comforting, exhorting, and glorifying towards someone else. Be careful not to participate in foolish talk with others. Let the words of your mouth and the meditation of your heart be acceptable to God. Ask God to cleanse your heart, because those bad things in your heart will eventually come out of your mouth. You must be alert to the tactics of the enemy and not allow him to cause you not to speak well of others. Good practice would be to think before you speak. You should see the beauty in every person you see, because God does. Remember, God is listening to our conversations.

Ask yourself this question: Would God be pleased with some of the things you are saying or thinking? The words you say matter, you can't take them back once spoken. Spend less time on the phone and in conversations with people who never have anything good to say. He is listening, so be wise with your words. In your TALK TIME WITH GOD ask Him to forgive you if you have fallen prey to this bad habit. God is not the author of confusion; Scripture warns you about taming your tongue. Our words can either bless or curse. Stay focused on the words you use. They matter.

Your Daily Prayer/Praise:

_____
_____
_____
_____
_____
_____
_____
_____
_____
_____
_____
_____

Your Daily Surrender:

_____
_____
_____
_____
_____
_____
_____
_____
_____
_____
_____
_____

Public Appearances

Leadership Workshops

Worship Leader

Psalmist

Worship Services

Speaking Engagements

Conferences Speaker/Preacher/Facilitator

Book Signing

To request Rev. Valarie W. Harris for an event please contact her at: TalkTimeVal@gmail.com

Thank you for your support!

About the Author

A native of Newport News, Virginia, Valarie was the only child of the late Howard and Rosa Williams. She is a wife, mother, grandmother, great grandmother, preacher, teacher, psalmist, worshiper, and writer whose greatest desire is to seek God's face and see others in the Body of Christ grow into an intimate relationship with the living Savior. She has a heart for those who desire a closer spiritual walk with God.

She is a 1971 graduate of George Washington Carver High School, who attained her B.S. degree from Norfolk State College in 1975. She has acquired many certificates in Computer Science and Technology from the University of Virginia, and she obtained her master's degree from Virginia Tech University in 2002. Valarie retired from the Hopewell Public School System after thirty-four years of teaching. Later she pursued a Worship Studies degree from Liberty University in 2016 and has taken numerous courses on Worship from The Kings University in Southlake, Texas. At this time, she is pursuing a Master of Divinity Degree from the Seraphim Ministries International Bible College.

Valarie has traveled with the Uniquely Chosen Hope Missions Team in 2017, 2018, and 2019 for Global Missions in Ghana, West Africa. She has also traveled to Mumbai, India, Puerto Rico, Amsterdam, London, Brussels, Paris, and various Caribbean islands.

The seed was planted to write this journal during her morning TALK TIME WITH GOD.

www.ingramcontent.com/pod-product-compliance
Lightning Source LLC
Chambersburg PA
CBHW052107070526
44584CB00017B/2370